STUDIES IN SOCIOLOGY

This series, prepared under the auspices ~~of the British Sociological~~ Association, is designed to provide short but comprehensive and scholarly treatments of key problem-areas in sociology. The books do not offer summary accounts of the current state of research in various fields, but seek rather to analyse matters which are the subject of controversy or debate. The series is designed to cover a broad range of topics, falling into three categories: (1) abstract problems of social theory and social philosophy; (2) interpretative questions posed by the writings of leading social theorists; (3) issues in empirical sociology. In addition, the series will carry translations of important writings in sociology which have not previously been available in English. Each book makes a substantive contribution to its particular topic, while at the same time giving the reader an indication of the main problems at issue; each carries an annotated bibliography, comprising a critical survey of relevant further literature.

ANTHONY GIDDENS

University of Cambridge

STUDIES IN SOCIOLOGY

General Editor: ANTHONY GIDDENS
Editorial Advisers: T. B. BOTTOMORE, DAVID LOCKWOOD and
ERNEST GELLNER

Published

POLITICS AND SOCIOLOGY IN THE THOUGHT OF MAX WEBER
Anthony Giddens

PROFESSIONS AND POWER
Terence J. Johnson

THE SOCIAL PROCESS OF INNOVATION: A STUDY IN THE SOCIOLOGY
OF SCIENCE
M. J. Mulkay

Forthcoming

THE SOCIOLOGY OF SOCIAL MOVEMENTS
J. Banks

MARXIST SOCIOLOGY
T. B. Bottomore

MATHEMATICS AND SOCIOLOGY
B. Hindess

STRIKES AND INDUSTRIAL CONFLICT
G. Ingham

THE DEVELOPMENT OF THE SOCIOLOGY OF KNOWLEDGE
S. Lukes

CONFLICT AND COHESION IN THE WESTERN WORKING CLASS
M. Mann

MICHELS AND THE CRITIQUE OF SOCIAL DEMOCRACY
F. Parkin

Politics and Sociology
in the Thought of Max Weber

ANTHONY GIDDENS
Lecturer in Sociology, University of Cambridge

Macmillan

First published 1972 by
THE MACMILLAN PRESS LTD
London and Basingstoke
Associated companies in New York Toronto
Dublin Melbourne Johannesburg and Madras

SBN 333 13436 2

Printed in Great Britain by
THE ANCHOR PRESS LTD
Tiptree, Essex

CONTENTS

ACKNOWLEDGEMENTS
AND BIBLIOGRAPHICAL NOTE

I should like to thank several persons who have read and commented helpfully on the first draft of this study: in particular, Martin Albrow, T. B. Bottomore, John Carroll and Steven Lukes.

References in the footnotes to works for which full details are given in the Bibliography simply quote author's name, date of the publication referred to, and page number where necessary, thus: Mommsen (1959) p. 118. All references which carry no author's name refer to works by Max Weber.

A. G.

1. INTRODUCTION

The past decade has witnessed a remarkable revival of scholarly interest in the writings of Max Weber. To paraphrase Erich Fromm's comment upon developments in Marxist scholarship, one might say that Weber has become transformed from a 'dead saint' into a 'living thinker'.[1] Today, opinions polarise about the contributions of Weber almost as completely as they do about those of Marx. The sharpest controversy over Weber's thought in the recent literature has concerned the relationship between his political and sociological writings.[2] In 1953, Georg Lukács published *Die Zerstörung der Vernunft* ('The Destruction of Reason'), a work which attempts to trace the development of irrationalism in German social thought from Schelling to Hitler. The book includes a section on Weber, in which Weber is treated as a prominent spokesman for the bourgeois imperialism of Wilhelmine Germany. Lukács's book, however, gives far more space to Nietzsche than it does to Weber, and the analysis of the writings of the latter is somewhat cursory. Although the work set something of the framework for the controversy which followed, the most important stimulus to debate was provided by Wolfgang Mommsen, in his *Max Weber und die deutsche Politik* ('Max Weber and German Politics'), published in 1959.

Mommsen's work is a detailed and closely documented study of Weber's political writings and involvements. The book places

[1] Erich Fromm, Foreword to T. B. Bottomore (ed.), *Karl Marx: Early Writings* (New York, 1964) p. i.

[2] For the most important relevant contributions, see Lukács (1955), Mommsen (1959, 1965), Roth (1965), Schmidt (1964) and Stammler (1971).

much stress upon Weber's commitment to the welfare of the German state as an ultimate political value, and, although somewhat critical of Lukács's analysis in this respect, insists strongly upon Weber's endorsement of German military imperialism. Although Mommsen does not discuss Weber's academic writings in detail, he seeks to draw various important lines of relationship between his political views and his academic works, tending to treat the latter often as something like direct ideological expressions of the former. Mommsen's book concludes with an analysis of the intellectual relationship between Weber's political writings and those of Carl Schmitt, thereby again linking aspects of Weber's work directly to the rise of fascism. On its appearance, Mommsen's work was heavily criticised for these interpretations by those whom he later referred to as the 'orthodox' adherents of Weber: in particular, Bendix, Löwenstein and Honigsheim. Although Mommsen himself was only marginally involved, the debate re-emerged, this time in a blunter and more extreme form, in the 1964 meetings of the German Sociological Association, held to commemorate the centenary of the birth of Max Weber.

These interchanges, whatever their own obvious political and ideological implications – which it is not my object to discuss in this study – have pushed to the forefront certain extremely significant questions, which hitherto have definitely not received the attention they deserve, concerning the social 'rooting' of Weber's sociology. One of the most urgent tasks confronting modern social theory is a reflexive one: that of re-examining the social and political environments which generated the main parameters of social thought which exist today. In the case of Weber, this means making something of a return to the sort of discussion which his works stimulated in Germany during his own lifetime. For most of his career Weber was a controversial figure, in both the academic and political worlds; and his contemporaries, of course, were very well aware that these two spheres of his activities were closely interconnected. But until a few years ago, most of the secondary literature on Weber – especially that which has appeared in English – has chosen to analyse his sociological studies in abstraction from his political views and involvements. It is entirely legitimate, of course, to sift the valid 'scientific' content from Weber's works, and to attempt to construct sociological theories which utilise some of his concepts and findings, and reject others. But in sociology, where the sort of cumulative formation of abstract theory characteristic of certain of the natural sciences is not possible, it is equally important to be conscious of the social and political context in which sociological theories come to be formulated. This in itself helps to offer, particularly in retrospect, a clearer perception of the elements in the ideas of a given thinker which are particularly 'time-bound'. However, there are additional gains to be made in examining some of the lines of interrelationship between Weber's political concerns and his academic works. Weber's writings cover an enormous span of fields in sociology, history, economics, jurisprudence and philosophy. Consequently, some of the leading secondary discussions of Weber's thought have stressed inconsistencies or discrepancies which are presumed to exist between the various parts of his life's work. But however diverse their substantive content, his works do have an intrinsic unity: the specific importance of Weber's political writings is that, far from adding to the apparent 'dispersal' of his interests, they provide an essential source of illumination of the continuity and coherence in his thought.

The primary aim of this study, therefore, is to elucidate some of the interconnections between Weber's political writings on the one hand, and his more academic contributions to the social sciences on the other. As a preface to the main part of the work, it will be useful to indicate a few of the important elements in his political and intellectual career. Max Weber was born in 1864, the son of a prominent politician, a member of the National Liberal Party. In her biography of her husband, Marianne Weber has described in some detail the richness of the influences which the young Weber experienced in his father's home. From an early age he came into contact with many of the leading figures in the Prussian political and academic worlds, including Treitschke, Kapp, Dilthey and Mommsen. His childhood spanned a period of years which was of decisive significance for German political development: the crucial phase in German history at which, under the leadership of Bismarck, the country at last became a centralised nation-state. The German victory over France in 1870–1 had an effect upon the Weber household which left a lasting emotional impact upon Max, although he was no more than six years old at the time.[3] While he never obtained political office, there was no point in his life at which political and academic interests did not intertwine in his personal experience. His youthful impressions of politics, filtered first through his father's circle and, as a young man, through the influence of his uncle, Hermann Baumgarten, produced in Weber an ambivalent orientation towards the achievements of Bismarck which he never fully resolved, and which lies at the origin of the whole of his political writings.

Weber's earliest academic writings concern legal and economic history. What appear to be purely technical, scholarly works, however – such as the dissertation on land tenure in ancient Rome, which Weber wrote in 1891 – actually held broader social and political implications in his thinking. In the thesis, Weber rejected the view, taken by some scholars of the day, that the economic history of Rome was a unique set of events, totally unamenable to analysis in terms of concepts derived from other situations; and he perceived in the social and economic structure of Rome some of the characteristics later to be discerned in the formation of capitalism in post-medieval Europe. Moreover, although he refused to accept some of the more specious comparisons which others had attempted to draw along these lines, the tensions which developed in the ancient world between the agrarian economy of large landed estates and emergent commerce and manufacture seemed to him to illuminate some of the problems facing contemporary Germany. He had the opportunity to confront these problems directly in a study, published in 1892, of the *Junker* estates to the east of the Elbe. This work formed part of a larger piece of research sponsored by the *Verein für Sozialpolitik*, investigating the conditions of land tenure in several main regions in Germany.[4] Through his affiliation to the *Verein*, a group of 'academic socialists' concerned with current social and political issues, Weber was able to participate in discussion and interchange of ideas with a number of younger economists and historians interested above all in the problems facing Germany in its transition to industrial capitalism. While the founder members of the *Verein*, the 'older generation' of economists such as

[3] Marianne Weber (1950) pp. 47–8.
[4] For a brief description, see Bendix (1966) pp. 14–48.

10

Wagner, Schmoller and Brentano, were interested primarily in questions connected with formulating policies of partial state intervention in economic life, the 'younger generation' – including, besides Weber, such authors as Sombart, Schulze-Gaevernitz and Tönnies – concerned themselves more broadly with the nature and origins of capitalism, and were heavily influenced by Marx.

Weber was appointed to a professorship of economics in Freiburg in 1894, and the following year delivered his *Antrittsrede* (inaugural lecture) there.[5] In the lecture, Weber developed some of the conclusions which he had reached in his study of agrarian conditions to the east of the Elbe, and related them specifically to the political and economic problems of Germany as a whole (see below, pp. 16–18). He gave particular attention to the so-called 'boundary problem' in the east. East Prussia, the homeland of the *Junker* landowners, had provided the springboard for the unification of Germany, and was the ultimate basis of Bismarck's power. But the position of the landed estates was becoming undermined by a burgeoning emigration of agricultural workers to other parts of Germany, attracted by the expansion of industrial production there. This situation was causing an influx of Polish workers from the east which, according to Weber, threatened the hegemony of German culture in those very areas where it had been strongest. Hence the influx of Poles must be stopped, and the eastern boundaries of Germany made secure. For Germany, he concluded, political and economic questions are inextricably linked; the country had forged its unity in conflict with other nations, and the maintenance and furtherance of its culture depended upon the continued assertion of its power as a bounded nation-state.

Weber did not develop the full implications of these views until later. For a period of several years, from 1897, he was incapacitated by an acute depressive disorder which forced him to abandon academic work altogether. While he did not return to university teaching until much later on in his life, he was able to resume his scholarly activities shortly after the turn of the century.

[5] 'Der Nationalstaat und die Volkswirtschaftspolitik' (1958*b*, pp. 1–25).

This period was the most productive of his career. He continued his studies of the *Junker* estates, but he was able for the first time to work out what had been latent in his earlier writings: a broad treatment of certain fundamental aspects of modern capitalist development, which found an initial statement in *The Protestant Ethic and the Spirit of Capitalism* (1904–5). At the same time he wrote and published essays dealing with the epistemology and methodology of the social sciences. These works undoubtedly both influenced and were influenced by a clarification of his political views which he attained during this period. In his *Antrittsrede* he had already set out a preliminary version of the 'leadership problem' facing Germany. The country had achieved unification in the political sphere while beginning to experience a rapid period of industrial development. *Junker* power had provided the main foundation for the achievement of political unity, but the future of Germany as a 'power-state' in Europe depended upon its becoming an industrialised state. Thus *Junker* domination, founded upon landownership, must be replaced by a new political leadership. But, as Weber had stated in 1895, neither the bourgeoisie nor the working class was as yet capable of providing that leadership. Bismarck had systematically fragmented and weakened the liberals; and he had stunted the leadership potential of the labour party, the Social Democrats, by passing the anti-socialist laws which, until they were repealed in 1890, had effectively placed the working class outside the political structure of the German state.

It became increasingly apparent to Weber, after the turn of the century, that the immediate future of Germany must lie with a sharpening of the political consciousness of the bourgeoisie. An inportant underlying motif of *The Protestant Ethic* was certainly that of identifying the historical sources of such a 'bourgeois consciousness'. The essays in epistemology and methodology which he wrote at this time also reflect political problems with which he was concerned, on a personal as well as an intellectual plane. Throughout his life, Weber was subject to two conflicting impulsions: towards the passive, disciplined life of the scholar, and towards the active and practical vocation of the politician. On the intellectual level, he sought to draw a clear-cut distinction between these two competing inspirations, recognising an abso-

12

lute dichotomy between the validation of 'factual' or 'scientific' knowledge on the one hand, and of 'normative' or 'value' judgements on the other. Hence, while the activity of the politician can be guided or informed by scientific knowledge of the kind established by history, economics or sociology, such knowledge can never ultimately validate the goals after which the political leader strives. This position had the effect of distancing Weber from the two major political movements competing with the liberals in Germany: the Conservative nationalists on the right, and the Marxist Social Democrats on the left. Each of these, in Weber's view, adhered to a 'normative' conception of history which they introduced into politics, claiming historical 'validation' of their right to rule.

In 1906 Weber also wrote two long essays on Russia, assessing the chances of the development of liberal democracy there following the first Russian Revolution. The so-called 'constitutional' government in Russia seemed to him as much of a sham as that in Germany, and for not altogether different reasons: in Russia, as in Germany, a politically conscious bourgeoisie had not yet emerged, and the country was still dominated by the traditional, agrarian elite. The question of the nature of the constitutional reforms required in Germany, if the necessary bourgeois political leadership were to be forthcoming, increasingly occupied Weber's attention during the years of the First World War, especially as it became apparent to him that Germany's military fortunes in the struggle were declining. In the period immediately before the outbreak of hostilities, and in the early part of the war, he wrote voluminously, producing his long essays on the 'world religions', Hinduism, Confucianism and Judaism, and a draft of *Economy and Society* (which was not published until after his death). But the war years brought to a head the tensions in German society which he had begun to analyse two decades earlier, and he gave over much of his time to the examination of political issues. He had for some while been strongly critical of what he once referred to as the 'hysterical vanity' of William II, and later on in the war changed from his previous advocacy of constitutional monarchy to arguing in favour of republicanism. In the two years prior to his death in 1920, he took up an active role in both the academic and political worlds. He accepted a pro-

fessorship at the University of Vienna, and gave a series of lec-
tures – a version of which has been subsequently published as
General Economic History[6] – in which he attempted to sum up
the major themes in his sociology of economic life and capitalist
development. Weber made a number of important political
speeches during the period of the German Revolution of 1918–19,
and narrowly missed selection as a parliamentary candidate for
the newly-formed Democratic Party. One of his last political
activities was as a member of the Commission which drafted the
Weimar Constitution.

[6] (1961).

2. MAIN THEMES IN WEBER'S POLITICAL WRITINGS

This study is divided into three principal sections. This section analyses the main elements in Weber's political standpoint at the various stages of his career. Section 3 examines the influence of his political involvements upon the structure and substance of his more academic works. Section 4 'reverses' this perspective, in order to specify how far his assessment of German politics was itself conditioned by the framework established in his other works.

Weber's writings in both politics and sociology have their roots in an attempt to analyse the conditions governing the expansion of industrial capitalism in Germany in the post-Bismarckian era. The background to this is well known to anyone with a cursory knowledge of German social history. For the greater part of the nineteenth century, Germany lagged behind both Britain and France in definite respects – especially in terms of its lack of political unification and, as compared to Britain particularly, in its relatively low level of industrial development. Moreover, when an integral German state did come into being, it was achieved under the leadership of Prussia, whose semi-feudal autocracy, founded upon the power of the *Junker* landowner, the civil service bureaucracy and the officer corps, contrasted considerably with the more liberalised constitutions and traditions of some of the southern German states. The full impact of industrial development, experienced during the closing decades of the nineteenth century, thus took place within the framework of a social and political order which was in important ways quite different from that characterising the emergence of capitalism in its 'classical' form : that is to say, in the case of Britain in the earlier part of the century. The Industrial Revolution in Britain took place in a society where prior developments had created a 'compromise'

15

social order in which, as Marx once expressed it, the aristocratic landowners 'rule officially', while the bourgeoisie 'in fact *dominate* all the various spheres of civil society'.[7] But in Germany, the liberal bourgeoisie did not engineer a 'successful' revolution. Germany achieved political unification as a consequence of Bismarck's promotion of an aggressively expansionist policy; and industrialisation was effected within a social structure in which power still devolved upon traditionally established elite groups.

When Weber began to take an active interest in politics, he found the liberal wing of the German bourgeoisie in decline, a phenomenon which could be directly traced to the results of Bismarck's domination.[8] In the face of the 'social question' or the 'red spectre' – the growth of the Social Democratic Party – the liberals opted for the security and economic prosperity seemingly offered by a continuing affiliation to conservative interests. Weber's *Antrittsrede* of 1895 contains his first systematic analysis of this situation. In the *Antrittsrede*, he sets himself firmly both against the proponents of an 'ethical' approach to politics, and against those who look to economic development to lead inevitably to the furtherance of political liberties:

> There can be no *peace* in the economic *struggle* for existence; only he who confuses appearance with reality can believe that the peaceful enjoyment of life is what the future holds for our descendants. . . . It is not for us to show our successors the way to peace and human contentment, but rather to show them the *eternal struggle* for the maintenance and cultivation of our national integrity.[9]

The lecture expresses a fervent advocacy of the interests of the 'power-state' as the necessary foundation of German politics. Germany has secured her unity through the assertion of her power

[7] Marx and Engels, *Werke* (Berlin, 1953) xi 95.

[8] The description of Weber's political writings given in this section is necessarily sketchy and somewhat slanted; a more lengthy treatment would take up issues which are largely excluded here. The reader seeking such an account should consult Mommsen's (1959) work.

[9] (1958*b*) pp. 12, 14.

in the face of international rivalry; the future of Germany thus lies with the preservation of the capacity of the nation to exert her will in international affairs. But the political leadership necessary to accomplish this, Weber asserts, is lacking. The creation of such a leadership is not merely a matter which depends upon the economic power of the various classes in German society:

> We ask whether they are *politically mature* : that is to say, whether they possess respectively the understanding and the capacity to place the political *power*-interests of the nation above all other considerations.[10]

The *Junkers*, Weber continues, are a declining class, who cannot continue to monopolise the political life of the country. But while it is 'dangerous' for an economically fading class to maintain political power, it is even more so if the classes which are acquiring an increasingly secure economic position aspire to national leadership without possessing the political maturity necessary to guide the fortunes of a modern state. Neither the working class nor the bourgeoisie as yet possess such a maturity. The working class is led by a collection of 'journalistic dilettantes', at the head of the Social Democratic Party : they have no organic connection with the class they claim to represent, and their revolutionary posture in fact acts against the further advancement of the working class towards political responsibility. The bourgeoisie remain timid and unpolitical; they long for the emergence of another 'Caesar' who will shelter them from the need to assume a leadership role. This is a consequence of their 'unpolitical past', which no amount of economic power in itself can replace. Weber concludes:

> The *threatening thing* in our situation . . . is that the bourgeois classes, as the bearers of the *power*-interests of the nation, seem to wilt away, while there are no signs that the workers are beginning to show the maturity to replace them. The danger does *not* . . . lie with the masses. It is not a question of the *economic* position of the *ruled*, but rather the *political* qualifi-

[10] Ibid., p. 18.

cation of the *ruling* and *ascending* classes which is the ultimate issue in the *social*-political problem.[11]

Thus, in 1895, Weber saw as the principal question affecting the future of Germany that of whether the economically prosperous bourgeoisie could develop a political consciousness adequate enough to undertake the leadership of the nation. The bulk of his subsequent political writings and actions can be interpreted as an attempt to stimulate the emergence of this liberal political consciousness in Germany. For Weber, this could not be achieved on 'ethical' grounds: there could be no question of refounding German liberalism upon a 'natural law' theory of democracy. He rejected, moreover, the classical conception of 'direct' democracy, in which the mass of the population participate in decision-making; this may be possible in small communities, but is quite irrelevant to the contemporary age. In the modern state, leadership must be the prerogative of a minority: this is an inescapable characteristic of modern times. Any idea 'that some form of "democracy" can destroy the "domination of men over other men" ' is utopian.[12] The development of democratic government necessarily depends upon the further advance of bureaucratic organisation.

According to Weber, the relationship between democracy and bureaucracy creates one of the most profound sources of tension in the modern social order. There is a basic antinomy between democracy and bureaucracy, because the growth of the abstract legal provisions which are necessary to implement democratic procedures themselves entail the creation of a new form of entrenched monopoly (the expansion of the control of bureaucratic officialdom). While the extension of democratic rights demands the growth of bureaucratic centralisation, however, the reverse does not follow. The historical example of ancient Egypt gives an illustration of this, involving as it does the total subordination of the population to a bureaucratised state apparatus. The existence of large-scale parties, then, which themselves are bureaucratic 'machines', is an unavoidable feature of a modern democratic

[11] Ibid., p. 23.
[12] Letter to Michels, 1908, quoted in Mommsen (1959) p. 392.

18

order; but if these parties are headed by leaders who have political expertise and initiative, the wholesale domination of bureaucratic officialdom can be avoided. Weber saw the likelihood of 'uncontrolled bureaucratic domination' as the greatest threat of the hiatus in political leadership left by Bismarck's fall from power. The development of representative democracy became for him the principal means whereby this could be avoided: 'there is only the choice: leadership-democracy (*Führerdemokratie*) with the "machine", or leaderless democracy – that is, the domination of "professional politicians" without a vocation, without the inner charismatic qualities that alone make a leader.'[13]

But for most of his life Weber found himself unable to identify wholly with any one of the organised political parties in Germany. At the turn of the century, several of the leading parties offered elements of what he sought, but none combined these elements in an acceptable way. He shared the nationalistic aspirations of the Conservative Party, but rejected both the 'mystic fervour' with which these were expressed, and the policy of giving economic support to the semi-feudal agrarian structure in the east. Neither of the two main liberal parties seemed to him to give any indication that they could overcome the lack of political inspiration analysed in the *Antrittsrede*. He accepted, with the National-Liberals (the right wing), the need for the expansion of industrial capitalism as necessary to the foundation of a modern economy; but the National-Liberals, through promoting protective tariffs, maintained close ties with Conservative interests, and continued to support the Prussian 'three-tier' system of suffrage in the face of Social Democratic demands for a democratic franchise. The Left-Liberals Weber regarded as having little appreciation of the 'power' characteristics of politics: their position was primarily based upon an 'ethical' support of democratic ideals of constitutional government, and consequently they posed no threat to the existing order.[14]

---

[13] (1958*b*) p. 532. 'In a democracy, the people choose a leader whom they trust; the leader who is chosen then says, "Now shut up and do what I say" ': quoted in Marianne Weber (1950) pp. 664–5.

[14] Ibid., p. 258. Weber considered the same to be true of the Naumann group; cf. Mayer (1956) pp. 45–6.

In this situation, it is inevitable that Weber should have felt drawn towards the Social Democratic Party (SPD): this was the only party of considerable political strength which was openly committed to a 'progressive' platform. Marianne Weber has written that Weber often considered joining the SPD; but he was effectively deterred from doing so by several basic factors in his assessment of the role of the party in German politics. He regarded what he saw as a dogmatic insistence upon Marxism on the part of the SPD leadership as one of the main elements producing the stagnation of German political development. The interests of bourgeoisie and working class, Weber held, were compatible for the foreseeable future : both stood to gain from the emergence of a fully industrialised German state. Moreover, if it were the case that the Social Democrats were to come to power by revolutionary means, the result would certainly be a vast expansion of bureaucratisation, since the economy would become centrally administered – Weber commented on several occasions that such an eventuality would produce a society which would be comparable to the bureaucratic state of ancient Egypt. But he was clear at an early date that the revolutionary ideology of the Social Democrats was markedly different from the actual interests of the party in German politics. This in itself provided ample evidence of the political naïveté of the party's leaders: the leadership of the party, according to Weber, was distinguished by its 'complacent innkeeper face, the visage of the petty bourgeois'.[15] His assessment of the SPD in 1907 is well conveyed in the following statement : 'What has most to fear in the long run, bourgeois society or Social Democracy? As concerns those elements within it which advance a *revolutionary ideology*, I believe it is the latter. It is now quite plain that there are definite conflicts with the Social Democratic bureaucracy. . . .' The more, he went on to say, the Social Democrats succeeded in becoming a recognised party, the more they would come to find that their 'revolutionary ardour' will be 'in great danger': 'We should see then that Social Democracy would never permanently conquer the towns or the state, but that, on the contrary, the state would conquer the Social Demo-

[15] *Gesammelte Aufsätze zur Soziologie und Sozialpolitik* (Tübingen, 1924) p. 409.

cratic Party.'[16] Thus he wrote to Michels in 1907 that he felt, at least for the immediate future, that there was little chance of his working together with the Social Democrats; while he was not officially affiliated to any party, he stood nearer to the bourgeois parties.

In the effects of the First World War upon German society, Weber saw both a vindication of his earlier analysis of the German social structure and the possibility of transforming the political order. For some time prior to 1914, he had foreseen the increasing likelihood of the outbreak of a major European conflict. Moreover, he made no secret of the positive sentiments which the 'great and wonderful' war inspired in him : the passivity, and the lack of a national political sense, which he had criticised in the past, were replaced by a collective assertion of the integrity of the nation in the face of the other world powers. But even in the midst of the early military successes, he was also pessimistic about the chances of a German victory. The most that could come out of the war, concerning Germany's position among the other European nations, could be the successful establishment of Germany as a recognised 'great power' in Central Europe – thus, in effect, finally bringing about what Bismarck had originally sought to attain. Most of Weber's attention, even from early on in the war, was in fact directed towards what could be achieved in changing the *internal* political structure of the country. Of the various political writings which he published towards the end of the war, the most important consisted in a number of articles first published in the *Frankfurter Zeitung* of 1917, later collected together as *Parlament und Regierung im neugeordneten Deutschland* ('Parliament and Government in a Reconstructed Germany'). Here he again deals with the 'Bismarckian legacy' – but in the context of the changes wrought by the war upon the character of German politics.

In *Parlament und Regierung*, on the basis of a sociological interpretation of German political institutions, Weber sets out an analysis of the conditions necessary to implement a parliamentary system in Germany which will be something more than what he previously referred to as the 'sham constitutionalism' of

[16] Ibid., p. 394.

the Wilhelmine era. The earlier forms of liberal and Social Democratic critique of government in Germany, for the most part, have been 'arrogant and extravagant', and have failed 'to understand the preconditions of effective parliaments'. But Weber still insists that the formation of a genuine parliamentary system is a necessity which is imposed by the position of the German national state, and is a means, not an end: 'For a rational politician the form of government appropriate at any given time is a technical question which depends upon the political tasks of the nation. . . . In themselves, technical changes in the form of government do not make a nation vigorous or happy or valuable. They can only remove technical obstacles and thus are merely means for a given end.' In every modern state, he reiterates, but especially in Germany, the main problem facing the formation of political leadership is that of controlling 'bureaucratic despotism'. The trend towards bureaucratisation, moreover, is characteristic of other institutions besides the state: decision-making increasingly becomes an 'administrative' matter, carried out according to the regularised precepts of 'experts'. Thus the modern military commander directs the conduct of battles from his desk. In industry, the private officialdom of white-collar employees increases in numbers relative to the proportion of manual workers. The bureaucratisation of the division of labour is founded in 'the "separation" of the worker from the material means of production, destruction, administration, academic research, and finance in general [which] is the common basis of the modern state, in its political, cultural and military sphere, and of the private capitalist economy'.[17] The significance of parliamentary government, according to Weber, is that it offers both the possibility of effective control of officialdom and a source for the education of political leaders. In holding that political leaders should be elected from within parliament, he looks, of course, to the British model. But parliament as a whole cannot 'rule' any more than the rank-and-file members of a modern political party can do so. As with the latter – and, indeed, with the mass of the population, who remain a 'passive' force in politics except at periods when they exercise their voting rights – members of parliament must

[17] Above quotations all from (1968) III 1381–94.

accept the leadership of a minority. A 'Caesarist' element is inseparable from the modern state; a party leader must possess the charismatic qualities necessary to acquire and maintain the mass popularity which brings electoral success. The 'plebiscitary' leader can use his charismatic appeal to initiate new policies and to depart from established bureaucratic procedure. It is a primary objective of parliament, however, to act as a safeguard against the excessive acquisition of personal power by a plebiscitary leader.

The existence of a functioning parliament is basic to the political training of leaders, through the skills developed in committee work and the framing of policy and legislation which is demanded of 'middle-level' professional politicians. But it is vital, Weber concludes, for parliamentary government to be grounded in a universal franchise. An enfranchised democratic order which lacks a firm parliamentary foundation will lead to an unchecked Caesarism – such as has tended to characterise French politics, in which the relative lack of organised party 'machines' has weakened parliamentary control. On the other hand, a parliamentary system which is not constituted through universal suffrage, so that leaders can emerge who command mass support, is likely to be subverted by the rule of officialdom. In Germany, a schism has been enforced between the electorate and party machinery on the one side, and the filling of high executive positions on the other. Those parliamentary leaders who have become ministers have had to resign their party affiliations : hence the talented political leaders have been drawn off, and have become executive officials outside of parliament itself. In *Deutschlands künftige Staatsform* ('The Future Form of the German State'), published towards the end of 1918, Weber argued that the president of the future German republic should be plebiscitary, elected by the mass of the population and not through parliament – a clause which eventually, partly under his influence, became written into the Weimar Constitution.[18]

Towards the latter years of the war, Weber witnessed the progressive disintegration of the national unity which the opening

[18] For Mommsen's analysis of the influence of these views on Carl Schmitt, cf. Mommsen (1959) pp. 404 ff. See also Weber, 'Der Reichspräsident', in (1958b).

of hostilities had fostered. The political divisions between right and left, which were temporarily bridged in the collective enthusiasm of 1914, began to open up again. Weber attributed this less to the activities of the revolutionary *Spartakus* group than to the intransigent position of Prussian-based conservatism. The deteriorating military and economic fortunes of Germany, culminating in 1918, led to a situation in which Weber's demands for the constitutional reorganisation of the German political system were achieved almost at one stroke – not within a state which had achieved the goal of enforcing its 'power-equality' with the other European countries, but as a nation in defeat. Weber's attitude towards the possibilities of setting up a socialist government as a result of the German Revolution is of some considerable interest, since this serves to underline the leading themes of his political analysis. Democratic government has come to Germany, he points out, not from the sort of 'successful struggle' which the bourgeoisie fought in Britain, but as a consequence of defeat. But the exigencies stated in the earlier political writings still stand : the political representatives of the bourgeois classes must assume responsibility for the future of Germany. The protection offered by the landed elite has finally been stripped away. In these circumstances, Weber believed, it will be possible and desirable to subject certain enterprises, such as insurance and mining, to state control. But a socialisation of the rest of the economy is definitely to be avoided. However great the default of the bourgeoisie in the past, especially the big industrialists, there is no other possible option open to Germany :

> We have truly no reason to love the lords of heavy industry. Indeed, it is one of the main tasks of democracy to break their destructive *political* influence. However, *economically* their leadership is not only indispensable, but becomes *more so* than ever *now*, when our whole economy and all its industrial enterprises will have to be organised anew. The *Communist Manifesto* quite correctly emphasised the *economically* (not the politically) *revolutionary* character of the work of the bourgeois-capitalist entrepreneur. No trade union, least of all a state-socialist official, can carry out these functions for us. We must simply make use of them, in their

right place : hold out to them their necessary premium – profits – without, however, allowing this to go to their heads. *Only* in this way – today! – is the advance of socialism possible.[19]

Weber scathingly denounced the activities of the extreme left in 1918 and 1919. While prepared to admit the feasibility of a restricted socialisation of the economy, he dismissed as an 'intox-ication' or a 'narcotic' the hopes for a radical transformation of society. Of the attempts to establish breakaway revolutionary states in Germany, he wrote to Lukács : 'I am absolutely con-vinced that these experiments can and will only bring discredit upon socialism for a hundred years.' In another context he re-marked : 'Liebknecht belongs in the madhouse and Rosa Luxem-burg in the zoological gardens.' The labour movement in Germany, he reiterated, can only have a future *within* a capitalist state. Underlying this assessment, of course, were the more general implications of the formation of a socialist society which Weber had previously elaborated – in particular, his anticipation of the bureaucratised state to which this would lead. But to this, in the context of a nation in military defeat and economic penury, he added other, more specific factors which would attend any attempt to establish a revolutionary regime. Only a bourgeois government could obtain the foreign credits necessary to econ-omic recovery; and, in any case, a revolutionary government would soon be overthrown by the military intervention of the victorious Western countries : this could lead subsequently to 'a reaction such as we have never yet experienced – and then the proletariat will have to count the cost'.[20]

The fact that Weber 'moved to the left' over the course of his political career has often been noted. In terms of the substantive policies which he advocated, this is undoubtedly true; but while shifting his specific political alignments, in fact he remained committed to a definite set of premisses which guided the whole of his political views. Although he later came to modify aspects of the views stated in the *Antrittsrede*, his inaugural lecture gives a preliminary statement of principles (some specific, others more general) which reappear in most of his subsequent political writ-

[19] (1958*b*) p. 448.

[20] Above quotations all from Mommsen (1959) pp. 303, 300, 284.

ings. These became more precisely formulated in the period following his recovery from his nervous breakdown: the same time at which he produced his first important methodological writings and *The Protestant Ethic and the Spirit of Capitalism*. Briefly stated, they consist of the following suppositions:

1. The most significant problems facing the German polity derive from the 'legacy of Bismarck': Germany has secured its political unification under the domination of a 'Caesar' whose downfall has left the new state with a dearth of capable political leadership.
2. The future of the German state depends upon its becoming a developed industrial power. The *Junker* 'aristocracy' is inevitably a declining class; but neither of the major classes created by capitalist development, the bourgeoisie and the working class, has generated the leadership capable of successfully promoting the interests of the German state. It is the bourgeoisie which must assume this task in the immediate future.
3. The threat of 'uncontrolled bureaucratic domination' is in no way to be resolved through the programmes of the revolutionary socialists, who presume that the bureaucratic state apparatus can be 'destroyed'; nor through the partial nationalisation schemes advocated by certain of the 'academic socialists'. All such programmes can only succeed in furthering the advance of bureaucracy.
4. The establishment of democratic government, no more than the projected future society of the revolutionary socialists, will neither abolish nor reduce the 'domination of man by man'. Democratic government, in a modern society, depends upon the existence of strictly bureaucratised 'mass' parties: however, in conjunction with the operation of parliament, these can create a leadership capable of independent initiative, which can thus guide the fortunes of the state.
5. The furtherance of the nation-state must take primacy over all other objectives. The interests of the German nation-state are the ultimate criteria according to which political policies are to be judged.

6. All politics, in the last analysis, involves struggles for power; there can be no final conclusion to such struggles. Hence any sort of approach to politics which is based purely upon universalistic ethical appeals (such as for 'freedom' or 'goodness') is futile.

3. THE POLITICAL CONTEXT OF WEBER'S SOCIOLOGY

It is often said that Weber's work represents a response to 'late' capitalism. Thus expressed, this is a misleading statement. What is specifically important as the political and economic background to Weber's sociological writings is, in fact, the *retardation* of German development.[21] Judged in terms of the British model, the concluding decades of the nineteenth century were indeed a period of 'mature' capitalist evolution : by 1900, Britain could be adjudged to have been 'industrialised' for more than half a century. Most sociologists in fact, when they speak generically of 'nineteenth-century capitalism', have in mind the case of Britain, which is treated as the exemplar of capitalist development. But the point is that the transition to capitalist industrialism took place in Germany only towards the latter part of the nineteenth century; it proceeded without the occurrence of a 'successful' bourgeois revolution, and in the framework of a process of political centralisation secured by Prussian military imperialism.

Weber's concern with 'capitalism', its presuppositions and consequences, in his sociological writings, thus has to be understood as an outcome, in large degree, of a preoccupation with the characteristics of the specific problems facing German society in the early phases of its industrial development. Such a concern underlies his study of the estates to the east of the Elbe. On its initial publication, the work received some considerable praise from conservative circles, because of its stance on the 'Polish question'.

[21] For an analysis of the problem of German 'backwardness' as related to the intellectual relationship between Marx and Weber, see Giddens (1970). A Marxist treatment of the development of German philosophy and sociology in this context is given in Lukács (1955).

But his more general observations in the study actually contain an appraisal of the declining economic position of the large land-owners; and this formed one main strand of his later political thinking. The 'feudal' agrarian structure in the east, which is the economic foundation of Prussia, will necessarily have to cede place to commercial capitalism.

Weber's analysis leads him to the conclusion, however, that neither the pre-existing hegemony of the *Junkers*, nor their declining position, can be explained in strictly economic terms. The *Junker* estates are not simply founded upon the economic 'exploitation' of the peasantry, but are spheres of political domination, rooted in strongly defined and traditional relationships of superordination and subordination. The military successes of Prussia, and her political accomplishments in Germany, Weber asserts, were attained on the basis of this traditionalistic power of the *Junkers*. But precisely because of their accomplishments in securing the unity of the German state, the *Junkers* have 'dug their own grave' : the political unification of the country which made Germany for the first time a major power-state in Central Europe, can henceforth be maintained only by the promotion of industrialisation. Only an industrialised state can hope to match the strength of the other Western countries – and will have the resources to meet what Weber, throughout his life, saw as the major threat in the east : Russia. In fact, Weber says, while they maintain 'aristocratic' pretensions, the *Junkers* have already effectively become commercialised land proprietors. Capitalism has

> gnawed at the social character of the *Junker* and his labourers. In the first half of the last century [i.e. the nineteenth century] the *Junker* was a rural patriarch. His farm hands, the farmers whose land he had appropriated, were by no means proletarians . . . they were, on a small scale, agriculturalists with a direct interest in their lord's husbandry. But they were expropriated by the rising valuation of the land; their lord withheld pasture and land, kept his grain, and paid them wages instead. Thus, the old community of interest was dissolved, and the farm hands became proletarians.

The result of the increasing undermining of the position of the *Instleute*, the bonded labourers, produced an emigration of workers from the east to the expanding industries of the western part of Germany. 'For Germany, all fateful questions of economic and social policy and of national interest are closely connected with this contrast between the rural society of the east and that of the west, and with its further development.'[22]

Weber's analysis of these issues differs considerably from that advanced in orthodox SPD circles at the turn of the century. Whereas Marxist authors sought to interpret the changing character of the agrarian east almost wholly in economic terms, Weber distinguished a complicated interplay of economic, political and ideological relationships. Thus, in explaining the emigration of labourers from the landed estates, Weber rejects the notion that this can be explained by reference to purely economic considerations: rather, the immediate driving force is a generalised notion of attaining 'freedom', from the restrictive ties of bonded labour. The ' "bread and butter question" ', Weber asserted, 'is of secondary importance'.[23]

The Protestant Ethic combines together, and projects on to a general level, several of the implications which Weber drew from his interpretation of the agrarian question and its relationship to German politics. It is misleading to regard the work, as many have, as a frontal attack upon historical materialism. Rather, the emergent line of Weber's reasoning, both in relation to the social structure of Germany, and on the more general intellectual plane, led him towards a standpoint which cut across the typical conceptions embodied in Marxism. His rejection of affiliations with the Social Democrats in the political sphere, while based upon his interpretation of the trends of development in German society, received an intellectual underpinning from acceptance of certain elements of the neo-Kantianism of the Heidelberg school.

[22] (1958a) pp. 382, 384. I have slightly amended the translation.
[23] *Die Verhältnisse der Landarbeiter im ostelbischen Deutschland* (Leipzig, 1892) p. 798. It is quite misleading to say, as Fleischmann does (1964, p. 194), that 'Weber conceived most of his major works with the aim of "verifying" the correctness of the Marxian theory of the relations between infrastructure and superstructure . . .'.

Weber's methodological position, as elaborated during the course of 1904–5, leans heavily upon Rickert, and upon the dichotomy between fact and value which is basic to the latter's philosophy. Weber used this to formulate a methodological critique both of idealism and Marxism, as overall schemes applied to history; on the level of political action, this underlay his rejection of Social Democracy, as representing an illegitimate fusion of ethical and political claims. As he once remarked of socialism, 'I *shall not* join *such* Churches'.[24]

To these methodological objections to Marxism, Weber conjoined his appraisal of the specific characteristics of the economic and political development of Germany. He agreed with certain elements of the conventional Marxist analysis of religious ideology, but none the less rejected that 'one-sided' historical materialism which allowed no positive influence to the symbolic content of specific forms of religious belief-system. Thus he accepted that 'The Church belongs to the conservative forces in European countries: first, the Roman Catholic Church . . . but also the Lutheran Church'. In Calvinism, however, he found a religious impulse which was not conservative, but revolutionary. While, as is shown in *The Protestant Ethic*, Lutheranism marked an important 'advance' over Catholicism in promoting the penetration of religious ethics into the sanctioning of rational labour in a 'calling', the Reformation did not, in itself, mark a radical break with traditionalism. On the whole, Lutheranism, like Catholicism, has acted to 'support the peasant, with his conservative way of life, against the domination of urban rationalist culture'. Both Churches consider that the personal ties pertaining between lord and serf can be more easily ethically controlled than the commercial relations of the market. 'Deep, historically conditioned contrasts, which have always separated Catholicism and Lutheranism from Calvinism, strengthen this anti-capitalistic attitude of the European Churches.'[25]

Thus, in seeking to identify the historical linkage between Calvinism and modern rational capitalism, Weber at the same time cast light upon the specific circumstances of the German

[24] Quoted in Baumgarten (1964) p. 607.
[25] Above quotations all from (1958*a*) pp. 370–1.

31

case. Calvinism, by sanctioning 'this-worldly asceticism', served to cut through the traditionalism which had characterised previous economic formations. Germany experienced the first 'religious revolution' of modern times, but Lutheranism was not the break with traditionalism which generated the ethical impulse which underlies modern capitalism. Instead, the Lutheran Church became the bulwark of a system of political domination which lasted into the twentieth century. In his political writings, Weber makes this point explicitly, pointing out a direct connection between Lutheranism and the growth of the Prussian state: '. . . Protestantism legitimated the state as a means of violence, as an absolute divine institution, and as the legitimate power-state in particular. Luther took from the individual the ethical responsibility for war and transferred it to the state authority; to obey this authority in all matters other than religious belief could never entail guilt.'[26]

Since it brought Weber into a confrontation with Marxist analyses of 'ideology' and 'superstructure', it was inevitable that much of the controversy about *The Protestant Ethic* should centre upon the 'role of ideas' in historical development. Weber himself scathingly dismissed the claims of historical materialism in this respect: the notion that systems of ideas can be in any sense 'ultimately' reduced to economic factors is 'utterly finished'; the truth is that there is no unilateral line of relationship between 'material' and 'ideal' factors. But standing behind the work is a more deeply rooted divergence from Marxism, concerning the essential structure of capitalism and bourgeois rationality; and in working out the implications of this standpoint, as elaborated in his studies of the non-European civilisations, Weber again took his point of departure from his interpretation of the German situation and 'Bismarck's legacy'.

A key theme in Weber's writings is his emphasis upon the independent influence of the 'political' as opposed to the 'economic'. Now it is important to recognise that each of the most significant forms of social-political theory originating in the earlier part of the nineteenth century – liberalism and Marxism – are in accord

---

[26] (1958*b*) pp. 543–4. My translation. A different version appears in (1958*a*) p. 124.

in minimising the influence of the state. The 'political' is seen as secondary and derived. Marxism does admit the importance of the state in capitalism, but regards it as expressing the asymmetry of class interests, and therefore as a social form which will 'disappear' when class society is transcended by socialism. Weber readily perceived the disjunction between this conception, as advanced by the spokesmen for the Social Democrats, and the realities of the social circumstances in which the Marxist party found itself. The SPD was certainly, especially during the period of the anti-socialist laws, 'outside' the state; but the only chance, as Weber saw it, which the party had of acquiring power was through the electoral system. However, the more it became successful in this way, according to his analysis, the more it was forced to become a bureaucratised, 'mass' party, which would become integrated with the existing state mechanism, and would no longer offer any 'alternative' to it. He rejected the standpoint of the Left-Liberals for similar reasons. The 1848 style of liberalism, in Weber's eyes, was obsolete in the context of the post-unification period in Germany. The assumptions underlying their standpoint – of the 'minimising' of political power through the full extension of rights of political franchise – was to Weber irreconcilable with the trend of development of German politics. Inside Germany, the main residue of Bismarck's domination was the existence of a bureaucratic state officialdom : a 'leaderless democracy' would be no advance over the present situation of the political hegemony of a doomed and declining class. Externally, Germany found itself surrounded by powerful states : the unification of Germany had been achieved through the assertion of Prussian military power in the face of the other major European nations. Thus, in becoming a 'bourgeois' society, Germany could not follow the same pattern as was shown by the political development of either Britain or the United States. On more than one occasion, Weber drew an explicit contrast between the historical circumstances of Germany and those of the United States. Germany had been placed in circumstances which 'have forced us to maintain the splendour of our old culture, so to speak, in an armed camp within a world bristling with arms'. The United States, on the other hand, 'does not yet know such problems', and 'will probably never encounter some of them'. The territorial isolation of the subcontinent which the United States occupies is 'the real historical seal imprinted upon its democratic institutions; without this acquisition, with powerful and warlike neighbours at its side, it would be forced to wear the coat of mail like ourselves, who constantly keep in the drawer of our desks the march order in case of war'.[27]

This assessment guided Weber in his general conceptualisation of the state and political power, as formulated in *Economy and Society*. In contrast to those contemporary thinkers (such as Durkheim) who regarded the modern nation-state primarily as a *moral* institution, Weber emphasises above all the capacity of the state to claim, through the use of force, a defined territorial area. The modern state is 'a compulsory association with a territorial basis', and monopolises, within its borders, legitimate control of the use of force. It is impossible, he held, to define a 'political' group (*Verband*) in terms of any definite category of ends which it serves: 'there is no conceivable end which *some* political association has not at some time pursued. And from the protection of personal security to the administration of justice, there is none which *all* have recognised.'[28] Thus the 'political' character of a group can only be defined in terms of its monopoly of the disposal of a force – which is a 'means' rather than an 'end'.

The organisation of the legal-rational state, in Weber's sociology, is applied to derive a general paradigm of the progression of the division of labour in modern capitalism. His application of this scheme, which is mediated by the conception of bureaucratisation, again expresses, in a definite sense, the independent character of the 'political' as compared to the 'economic'. For Marx, and for most nineteenth-century social thought generally, the problem of bureaucracy is given little prominence – a fact which is to be traced directly to the treatment of political organisation as heavily dependent upon economic power (class domination). Weber does not deny, of course, that modern capitalism involves the emergence of a class system based upon

[27] (1958a) pp. 384–5.
[28] (1968) I 55–6.

capital and wage-labour. But this is not for him, as it was for Marx, the main structural axis of the increasing differentiation of the division of labour which accompanies the advance of capitalism. Rather than generalising from the economic to the political, Weber generalises from the political to the economic: bureaucratic specialisation of tasks (which is, first and foremost, the characteristic of the legal-rational state) is treated as the most integral feature of capitalism. Thus Weber rejects the conception that the expropriation of the worker from his means of production has been confined to the economic sphere alone; any form of organisation having a hierarchy of authority can become subject to a process of 'expropriation'. In the modern state, 'expert officialdom, based on the division of labour' is wholly expropriated from possession of its means of administration. 'In the contemporary "state" – and this is essential for the concept of state – the "separation" of the administrative staff, of the administrative officials, and of the workers from the material means of administrative organisation is completed.'[29]

At this point, Weber's analysis of the political development of Germany rejoins his general conception of the growth of Western capitalism and the likely consequences of the emergence of socialist societies in Europe. The specific 'problem' of German political development is that of the 'legacy' of Bismarck, which has left Germany with a strongly centralised bureaucracy that is not complemented by an institutional order which can generate an independent political leadership, as is demanded by the 'tasks of the nation'. Such a political leadership, provided in the past by the Prussian aristocracy, can no longer be derived from this source in a capitalist society. This leaves the working class and the bourgeoisie. Both Weber's analysis of the specific characteristics of the SPD, and his generalised formulation of the growth of the bureaucratised division of labour in capitalism, reinforce his conviction that a bourgeois constitution is the only feasible option for Germany. The ideological impetus of the Social Democrats, fostering the notion that the bureaucratic apparatus of the state could be overthrown and destroyed by revolutionary means, he considered simply as fantasy. Not only is it the case that a

[29] (1958a) p. 82.

capitalist economy necessitates bureaucratic organisation, but the socialisation of the economy would inevitably entail the further spread of bureaucracy, in order to co-ordinate production according to central 'planning'. On the more general level, this conclusion is reached via the analysis of the process of 'expropriation' in the division of labour. The Marxist anticipation of socialism is grounded in the belief that capitalist society can be transcended by a new social order; but in Weber's conception, the possibility of the transcendence of capitalism is completely eliminated. The essential character of capitalism is not given in the class relationship between wage-labour and capital, but in the rational orientation of productive activity. The process of the 'separation' of the worker from his means of production is only one instance of a process of the rationalisation of conduct which advances in all spheres of modern society. This process, giving rise to bureaucratic specialisation, is irreversible. Since socialism is predicated upon the further imposition of rational control of economic conduct (the centralisation of the economy), and upon the 'disappearance' of the 'political' through its merging with the 'economic' (state control of economic enterprises), the result could only be an enormous expansion in bureaucratisation. This would not be the 'dictatorship of the proletariat', but the 'dictatorship of the official'.[30]

Weber's analysis of the political structure of Germany is concerned with the interplay of three main elements: the position of the traditionally established 'feudal' *Junker* landowners; the tendency towards 'uncontrolled bureaucratic domination' by the state officialdom; and the dearth of political leadership bound up with each of these factors. These three components reappear on the more general level in Weber's political sociology, in his typology of domination: traditional, legal and charismatic. The domination of the *Junkers* undoubtedly served him as the proximate model (together with the case of Rome, which he used as offering certain comparisons with Germany in his early writings) in drawing out the general implications of the contrast between the 'pure types' of traditional and legal domination, and the relationship between both and economic activity. 'The domina-

[30] *Gesammelte Aufsätze zur Soziologie und Sozialpolitik*, p. 508.

tion of a feudal stratum tends,' Weber made clear, 'because the structure of feudalised powers of government is normally predominantly patrimonial, to set rigid limits to the freedom of acquisitive activity and the development of markets.'[31] But in common with his general emphasis, he stressed that it is the administrative practices of traditional domination, rather than their purely economic policy, which inhibits the growth of rational capitalistic activity. Of particular significance here is the 'arbitrary' character of traditional administration, which militates against the emergence of formal rationality or 'calculability' in social action. The historical circumstances of Western Europe, according to Weber, are unique in having fostered the development of the rational state, with its expert officialdom. This has been one major condition (among others) which has facilitated the rise of modern capitalism in the West.

The case of Germany, however, shows that the growth of the rational state is in no sense a sufficient condition for the emergence of modern capitalism. In the countries in which capitalism came into being at an early date, England and Holland, the bureaucratic state has been less developed than in Germany. It is the existence of a bureaucratic state in Germany, and the specific direction in which it was channelled under Bismarck, which has left the country in the hands of politicians 'without a calling'. 'Professional politicians', as Weber demonstrates in his studies of the Eastern civilisations, have emerged in all developed patrimonial states. These are individuals who have come to prominence in the service of a king : 'men who, unlike the charismatic leader, have not wished to be lords themselves, but who have entered the *service* of political lords.' But only in the West have there been professional politicians whose lives have been devoted to 'the service of powers other than the princes'; who live 'off' politics, and who recognise only the legitimacy of impersonal legal principles. The development of this process occurred in Europe in different ways in different places, but has always involved the eventual development of a struggle for power between the king and the administrative staff which had grown up around him. In Germany, this took a particular form :

[31] (1968) I 239. Amended translation.

Wherever the dynasties retained actual power in their hands –
as was especially the case in Germany – the interests of the
prince were joined with those of officialdom *against* parliament
and its claims for power. The officials were also interested in
having leading positions, that is, ministerial positions, occupied by their own ranks, thus making these positions an object
of the official career. The monarch, on his part, was interested
in being able to appoint the ministers from the ranks of devoted
officials according to his own discretion. Both parties, however,
were interested in seeing the political leadership confront
parliament in a unified and solidary fashion. . . .[32]

All modern states, of course, involve these two forms of officials :
'administrative' and 'political' officials. Weber's discussion of the
relationship between these two forms of modern officialdom in
Germany is based upon analysis of the qualities of political
leadership which is directly connected with his formulation of
charismatic domination in general. The bureaucratic official must
carry out his duties in an impartial fashion : as Weber frequently
said, *sine ira et studio*. The political leader, by contrast, must 'take
a stand' and 'be passionate'. The 'routinisation' of politics – that
is to say, the transformation of political decisions into decisions of
administrative routine, through domination by bureaucratic
officialdom – is specifically foreign to the demands which are most
basic to political action. This phenomenon, which occupied much
of Weber's attention in his analysis of the lack of political leadership in Germany, forms a major component of his generalised
comparison of charisma with both traditional and rational-legal
domination. Charisma is, as a 'pure type', wholly opposed to the
routine, the *alltäglich*. Traditional and legal domination, on the
other hand, are both forms of everyday administration, the one
being tied to precedents transmitted from previous generations,
the other being bound by abstractly formulated universal principles. The charismatic leader, 'like . . . every true leader in this
sense, preaches, creates, or demands *new* obligations'.[33] It is for

[32] (1958a) pp. 83, 89–90. Weber contrasts this, as he often does,
with the development of politics in England, 'where parliament
gained supremacy over the monarch'.

[33] (1968) I 243.

this reason that the 'charismatic element' is of vital significance in a modern democratic order; without it, no consistent policy-making is possible, and the state relapses into leaderless democracy, the rule of professional politicians without a calling.

4. THE SOCIOLOGICAL FRAMEWORK OF WEBER'S POLITICAL THOUGHT

The preceding section of this study has sought to identify some of the principal lines of connection between Weber's political writings and his general sociological works, placing the emphasis upon those aspects of his sociology which were most directly influenced by his analysis of the political development of Wilhelmine Germany. The influence of 'the German model' on Weber's thinking was profound : virtually all of his major intellectual interests were shaped by it. But his evaluation of the political development of Germany was also brought into sharper focus, and more systematically formulated, within the abstract framework of thought which he worked out from the turn of the century onwards. The methodological position which he established at the outset of this period is particularly important in this connection. As with other parts of his works, the tendency has been – again, particularly in the English-speaking world – to emphasise the existence of a disjunction between his methodological essays on the one hand, and his more empirical writings on the other. However, as Löwith has emphasised, Weber's methodological standpoint is inseparable from his other works, and more particularly from his general interpretation of the rise of modern capitalism. The main elements of Weber's methodological views were elaborated at the same time as he was working on *The Protestant Ethic*; and these views were a major intellectual 'input', helping to mould his analysis of the trend of development of Western capitalism in general, and of the German social and political structure in particular.[34]

[34] There are undoubtedly important *psychological* connections between the characteristics of Weber's personality and the methodological position which he adopted. As Mommsen has remarked,

Weber's methodological essays are heavily polemical in character, and have to be seen against the background of the various schools of social and economic thought in nineteenth-century Germany. In his lengthy essay on Roscher and Knies, he deals with two sets of overlapping problems: the confusion, in the works of these writers, of commitment to rigorous empirical method with the use of 'mystical' concepts adopted from classical idealist philosophy; and the question of the supposed 'irrational subjectivity' of human behaviour compared to the 'predictability' of the natural world. Human conduct, Weber asserts, is as 'predictable' as are events in the natural world: 'The "predictability" (*Berechnenbarkeit*) of "processes of nature", such as in the sphere of "weather forecasts", is not nearly so "certain" as the "calculation" of the actions of someone known to us. . . .'[35] Thus 'irrationality' (in the sense of 'free will' = 'incalculability') is by no means a specific component of human conduct: on the contrary, such irrationality, Weber concluded, is 'abnormal', since it is a property of the behaviour of those individuals who are designated as 'insane'. It is thus fallacious to suppose that human actions are not amenable to generalisation; indeed, social life depends upon regularities in human conduct, such that one individual can calculate the probable responses of another to his own actions. But, equally, this does not imply that human actions can be treated wholly on a par with events in the natural world – that is, as 'objective' phenomena, in the way assumed by positivism. Action has a 'subjective' content not shared by the world of nature, and the interpretative grasp of the meaning of actions to the actor is essential to the explanation of the regularities discernible in human conduct. For this reason, Weber insists that the individual is the 'atom' of sociology: any proposition involving reference to a collectivity, such as a party or a nation, must ultimately be

Weber's 'whole scientific work, his uncompromising striving for intellectual integrity and scientific objectivity, can be seen in a certain sense as a continual, grandiose attempt to secure for himself distance and inner freedom in relation to practical political events' : Mommsen (1959) p. 1. For a recent analysis along these lines, see Mitzman (1970).

[35] *Gesammelte Aufsätze zur Wissenschaftslehre* (Tübingen, 1965) p. 64.

41

resolvable into concepts which refer to the actions of individual men.

The position which Weber adopts in these respects, then, refuses to identify 'free will' with the irrational. Human actions which are propelled by such forces are governed by the very opposite of freedom of choice : the latter is given to the degree to which conduct approximates to 'rationality', which signifies here the correspondence of means to ends in motivated action. Hence he identifies the two pure types of rational action, each of which is 'intelligible' to the social scientist in terms of means–ends relationships : 'purposeful rationality' (*Zweckrationalität*), in which the actor rationally assesses the full range of consequences entailed by the selection of a given means to achieve a particular end, and 'value-rationality', in which an individual consciously pursues one overriding end with single-minded devotion, without 'counting the cost'. Both of these Weber contrasts with irrational action, and sets up as a basic methodological tenet the prescription that 'all irrational, affectually determined elements of behaviour' should be treated 'as factors of deviation from a conceptually pure type of rational action'.[36]

It is important to emphasise that, according to this methodological scheme, the 'moral' is logically quite separate from the 'rational'. The assessment of rationality takes moral objectives or 'ends' as *givens*; Weber wholly rejects the conception that the sphere of the 'rational' can extend to the evaluation of competing ethical standards. What he often refers to as the 'ethical irrationality of the world' is fundamental to his epistemology. Statements of fact, and judgements of value, are separated by an absolute logical gulf : there is no way in which scientific rationalism can provide a validation of one ethical ideal compared to another. The unending conflict of divergent ethical systems can never be resolved by the growth of rational knowledge. It follows that what is 'worth' knowing cannot itself be determined rationally, but must rest upon values which specify why certain phenomena are 'of interest' : the objective investigation of human action is possible, but only on the prior basis of the selection of problems which have value-relevance.

[36] (1968) i 6.

Weber's methodological standpoint thus hinges upon the establishment of certain polarities between 'subjectivity' and 'objectivity', and between 'rationality' and 'irrationality' :

> The *objective* validity of all empirical knowledge rests exclusively upon the ordering of the given reality according to categories which are *subjective* in a specific sense, namely, in that they present the *presuppositions* of our knowledge and are based on the presupposition of the *value* of those *truths* which empirical knowledge alone is able to give us. . . . But these data can never become the foundation for the empirically impossible proof of the validity of the evaluative ideas. The belief which we all have in some form or other, in the meta-empirical validity of ultimate and final values, in which the meaning of our existence is rooted, is not incompatible with the incessant changefulness of the concrete viewpoints, from which empirical reality gets its significance. Both these views are, on the contrary, in harmony with each other. Life with its irrational reality and its store of possible meanings is inexhaustible.[37]

Hence for Weber, there can be no sense in which history can be 'rational', as postulated by either Hegelian 'objective idealism', or by Marxism, whereby the social development of man unfolds a progression towards the attainment of rationally determined ideals. Marx's statement that 'Mankind always sets itself only such tasks as it can solve' is as antithetical to Weber's position as is Hegel's famous proposition that 'what is rational is actual, and what is actual is rational'. As Weber sometimes expresses it, truth and goodness stand in no definite historical relationship to each other.

This epistemological position has consequences in Weber's sociological and political thought which extend far beyond the immediate sphere of the methodology of the social sciences. The 'ethical irrationality' of the world is a major element in the con-

[37] (1949) pp. 110–11. The polarisation between the 'rational' and 'irrational' (in the various senses in which Weber uses these terms) tends to preclude a recognition of any distinction between the '*non*-rational' and the 'irrational'.

ceptions underlying his studies of the 'world religions', and in his analysis of the specific path of development taken by rationalisation in the West. According to Weber's standpoint, there can never be a rational solution to the competing ethical standards which exist: all civilisations thus face the problem of 'making sense' of the 'irrationality' of the world. Religious theodicy provides a 'solution' to this problem, and the need to 'make sense of the senseless' is a main psychological impetus towards the rationalisation of systems of religious beliefs. The growth of rationalisation depends upon forces *which are not themselves rational*; hence the importance of charisma in Weber's thought. Charisma is 'specifically irrational' force, in that it is 'foreign to all rules'.[38] It is this which makes charismatic movements the major revolutionary element in history, the most potent source of new forms of rationalisation.

Weber's concept of 'rationalisation' is a complex one, and he uses the term to cover three sets of related phenomena: (1) What he variously refers to (from its positive aspect) as the 'intellectualisation' or (from its negative aspect) as the 'disenchantment' (*Entzauberung*) of the world. (2) The growth of rationality in the sense of 'the methodical attainment of a definitely given and practical end by the use of an increasingly precise calculation of adequate means'.[39] (3) The growth of rationality in the sense of the formation of 'ethics that are systematically and unambiguously oriented to fixed goals'. As he shows in his studies of India and China, the rationalisation of systems of ultimate beliefs may take numerous different forms, involving various combinations of these three elements. The specific form of social and economic development of Western Europe embodies a combination which is, in certain definite ways, quite distinct from the directions which rationalisation has taken elsewhere.

Weber details several major spheres of social and economic life in which rationalisation had proceeded in a specific way, or to an advanced degree, in the West, even prior to the advent of modern capitalism. These prior developments – such as the formation of rational jurisprudence inherited from Roman law – played a

[38] (1968) I 244.
[39] (1958a) pp. 293–4. Amended translation.

definite role in facilitating the rise of contemporary capitalism. The importance of Calvinism and other branches of ascetic Protestantism, as Weber makes clear in *The Protestant Ethic*, is not that it was a 'cause' of the rise of modern capitalism, but that it provided an *irrational* impetus to the disciplined pursuit of monetary gain in a specified 'calling' – and thereby laid the way open to the further spread of the distinctive types of rationalisation of activity stimulated by the voracious expansion of capitalism. Ascetic Protestantism sanctioned the division of labour which is integral to modern capitalism, and which inevitably conjoins the spread of capitalism to the advance of bureaucracy. The bureaucratised division of labour, which, with the further development of capitalism, becomes characteristic of all major social institutions, henceforth functions 'mechanically', and has no need of the religious ethic in which it was originally grounded. The further expansion of capitalism thus completes the disenchantment of the world (through a commitment to scientific 'progress'); transmutes most forms of social relationship into conduct which approximates to the *Zweckrational* type (through the rational co-ordination of tasks in bureaucratic organisations); and advances the spread of norms of an abstract, legal type which, principally as embodied in the state, constitute the main form of modern 'legitimate order'.

Each of these three aspects of the rationalisation promoted by capitalism has consequences to which Weber attributed an essential significance in analysing the modern political order:

1. Since Weber establishes as a logical principle that scientific propositions or empirical knowledge cannot validate judgements of value, it follows that the growth of scientific intellectualisation which is characteristic of capitalism cannot, in and of itself, confer meaning. Thus the very progress of science, he concludes, has dispelled the view which once promoted scientific endeavour:

> To artistic experimenters of the type of Leonardo and the musical innovators, science meant the path to *true* art, and that meant for them the path to true *nature*. . . . And today? Who – aside from certain big children who are indeed found in the natural science – still believes that the findings of astron-

omy, biology, physics, or chemistry could teach us anything about the *meaning* of the world. . . . If these natural sciences lead to anything in this way, they are apt to make the belief that there is such a thing as the 'meaning' of the universe die out at its very roots.[40]

A stress upon the necessity of facing up 'without illusions' to the realities of the modern world is a constant theme of Weber's political writings. 'Whosoever . . . wishes to carry on politics on this earth must above all things be free of illusions. . . .'[41] This theme is itself closely integrated with his conception of the 'ethical irrationality' of the world. The creation of a sphere of rational political activity, freed from the penetration of gods, spirits or the trappings of traditional symbols, makes plain the irremediable power conflicts which are the essence of politics. The consequence of the disenchantment of the world is that the trans-cendental values which confer meaning otherwise exist only in 'the brotherliness of direct and personal human relations', or become projected into forms of mystic withdrawal. Those individuals who cannot 'face the fate of the times' can take refuge in such withdrawal, either into the traditional churches, or into one of the newer cults. But such men thereby forfeit the capacity to participate directly in politics. Those who look to the transcendence of human conflict through the medium of politics, who seek to attain an end to the 'domination of man by man', are in flight from reality as much as those who abandon public life in favour of mystic retreat : hence Weber's scathing critique of the 'radical illusionists' in politics – the revolutionary socialists – 'who would like to strike down every independent man who tells them uncomfortable truths . . .'.[42] He 'who wishes to live as modern man', even if this be 'only in the sense that he has his daily paper, railways, electricity, etc.', must resign himself to the loss of ideals of radical revolutionary change : indeed he must abandon 'the *conceivability* of such a goal'.[43]

[40] Ibid., p. 142.
[41] (1958*b*) p. 28.
[42] Ibid., p. 470.
[43] Quoted in Mommsen (1959) p. 118.

The active politician, therefore, according to Weber, needs 'passion in the sense of *matter-of-factness*', the *Alltagweisheit* which balances devotion to a 'cause' with an awareness of the ever-present tension between means and ends, and of the 'paradox of consequences'. It is this awareness which is lacking among the revolutionaries, who fail to see that the *means* which have to be used to reach their goal must bring about a state of affairs which is quite discrepant from their stated end. Thus the Bolshevik government in Russia, Weber wrote in 1918, is simply a military dictatorship of the left, no different in content from dictatorship of the right, except that it is a 'dictatorship of *corporals*' rather than of generals.[44] The problem of the 'paradox of consequences', of course, is at the root of Weber's differentiation between the 'ethic of responsibility' and the 'ethic of conviction' (*Gesinnsungsethik*), which corresponds, on the level of ethics, to the distinction between purposeful and value rationality. It follows from Weber's own logical standpoint that the adherent of an ethic of ultimate ends in politics cannot be *shown*, by rational demonstration, that he is mistaken in pursuing the course of action which he does; but such a man is one who 'cannot stand up under the ethical irrationality of the world', who has no awareness of the 'daemonic' character of political power.

2. The intellectualisation characteristic of modern capitalism, according to Weber, is intimately bound up with the rationalism of human conduct in the second sense, especially as this manifests itself in the bureaucratised division of labour. In both his sociological and political writings, he identifies the advance of bureaucratic rationality as an inevitable component of the growth of capitalism: the 'alienative' effects of the modern social order, which Marx traced to the character of the class system in capitalist production, are in fact derivative of bureaucratisation. Weber often used the imagery of the machine in analysing the nature of bureaucratic organisation. Like a machine, bureaucracy is the most rational system of harnessing energies to the fulfilment of specified tasks. The member of a bureaucracy 'is only a single cog in an ever-moving mechanism which prescribes to him an essentially fixed route of march'. A bureaucracy, in common with a

[44] (1958*b*) pp. 280–1.

machine, can be placed in the service of many different masters. Moreover, a bureaucratic organisation functions efficiently to the degree that its members are 'dehumanised': bureaucracy 'develops the more perfectly . . . the more completely it succeeds in eliminating from official business love, hatred, and all purely personal, irrational, and emotional elements which escape calculation'.[45]

But, according to Weber, there can be no possibility of transcending the subordination of individuals to the specialisation of tasks entailed in bureaucratisation. The advance of bureaucracy imprisons man in the *Gehäuse der Hörigkeit*, the 'iron cage' of the specialised division of labour upon which the administration of the modern social and economic order depends. *The Protestant Ethic* ends with a striking exposition of this:

> Limitation to specialised work, with a renunciation of the Faustian universality of man which it involves, is a condition of any valuable work in the modern world; hence deeds and renunciation inevitably condition each other today. . . . The Puritan wanted to work in a calling; we are forced to do so. For when asceticism was carried out of monastic cells into everyday life, and began to dominate worldly morality, it did its part in building the tremendous cosmos of the modern economic order. This order is now bound to the technical and economic conditions of machine production which today determine the lives of all the individuals who are born into this mechanism, not only those directly concerned with economic acquisition, with irresistible force.[46]

In Weber's view, both conservatives and socialists share in common the misconceived belief that it is possible for modern man to 'escape from the cage': the former look to a reversion to a previous age, the latter to the formation of a new form of society which will radically change the existing conditions of capitalist production. Both have in mind the 'universal man' of humanist

[45] (1968) iii 998, 975.
[46] *The Protestant Ethic and the Spirit of Capitalism* (New York, 1958) pp. 180–1.

culture, and anticipate the disappearance of the 'fragmented specialisation' of the capitalist division of labour. But this culture is irretrievably destroyed by bureaucratisation. The ideal of the 'universal man' provided a substantive goal of education in systems of patrimonialism in which administrative tasks manifested only a low level of rationalisation. Qualification for office in those circumstances could be based upon the conception of the 'cultivated personality': a man of all-round competence, whose educational attainments were primarily demonstrated in his demeanour and bearing, rather than in the possession of specialised skills. Today, however, in education as in social life generally, specialisation is unavoidable, and professional education replaces humanism.

It is these considerations which underlie his famous discussion of 'ethical neutrality'. The professors of the 'old school', such as Schmoller, belong to the time when Germany stood on the threshold of its capitalist development, a time when it was usual to 'assign to the universities and thereby to themselves the universal role of moulding human beings, of inculcating political, ethical, aesthetic, cultural or other attitudes . . .'. According to Weber – and this, of course, following his standpoint, cannot be rationally proved, since it entails a judgement of value – this conception should be abandoned in favour of one which regards the university as having 'a really valuable influence only through specialised training by specially qualified persons'. It follows from the latter viewpoint, Weber holds, that 'intellectual integrity' should be the only general objective which is promoted in the lecture-hall. Thus discipline and self-limitation, the characteristic properties of a modern 'calling', have to apply to the position of professor (and of student) as much as any other modern occupation. The professor, therefore, should confine himself within the university setting, to the rigorous exposition of the subject which he is specially qualified to teach. The charismatic properties of professorial personalities should be excluded as far as possible from influencing their teaching: 'Every professional task has its own "inherent norms" and should be fulfilled accordingly. . . . We deprive the word "vocation" (Beruf) of the only meaning which still retains ethical significance if we fail to carry out that specific kind of self-restraint which it requires.' The 'dilettante', a term Weber uses so frequently as a derogatory epithet, is precisely one who fails to perform his 'calling' in a disciplined fashion, and who instead lays claim to a universal competence which he cannot possess.

Weber favoured the completion of the process of the internal rationalisation of university education only in order to emphasise more fully the need to recognise politics as the all-important area in modern social life in which the 'war of the competing gods' should be legitimately carried on. The maintenance of the assumption that the university provides a proper platform for the dissemination of value-judgements was to Weber a manifestation of the continuing power of conservative circles over university education. He himself witnessed the retardation of the careers of some of his friends, notably Michels and Simmel, as a result of strictly non-intellectual considerations – Michels because he was a Social Democrat, and Simmel because he was a Jew. The conception which allows that the university chair may be used to advance value-positions is only tenable if all points of view are represented; this is patently not the case where 'the university is a state institution for the training of "loyal" administrators'.[47]

3. The growth of what Weber sometimes terms 'technical rationality' in the West, as evinced in social relationships in the form of bureaucratisation, is, of course, necessarily closely tied to the development of rationalised norms of the 'legal' type (i.e. to rationalisation in the third sense). It is difficult to overstress the significance which Weber placed upon the development of rational law in his analysis of modern capitalism. The importance of the heritage of Roman law in Western Europe is not that it was directly incorporated into the institutions which gave rise to rational capitalism, but is to be traced to the fact that it was a main element in the creation of formally rational juristic thought. In every type of absolutist or hierocratic administration the enforcement of juridical process is based upon substantive criteria of procedure which are not applied as formal 'principles'. Law is administered either arbitrarily from case to case, or according to tradition. The rise of rational law thus signals the diminishing

[47] Above quotations from (1949) pp. 3, 6, 7.

power of such traditional systems of domination. The affinity between capitalist production and rational law derives from the factor of 'calculability' which is intrinsic to both. In the West, and nowhere else, this relationship, in significant degree, has been mediated by the state. The creation of the corpus of rational law in the West 'was achieved through the alliance between the modern state and the jurists for the purpose of making good its claims to power'.[48]

The abstract categorisation of the pure type of 'legal domination' which forms part of *Economy and Society* is directly integrated with Weber's analysis of the rise of the rational state. He did not live to complete the systematic treatment of the modern state which he planned to write, and while his writings refer at many points to the distinctive features of the Western form of the state, these are nowhere treated at length. Thus some of the general propositions underlying his conception of rational legal domination, as manifest in the modern state, have to be reconstructed from a diverse range of materials. One such proposition concerns the *limits* of legal domination. It is of basic importance to Weber's analysis of the modern state that, as he expresses it, 'no domination is *only* bureaucratic, that is, is only led by a contractually employed and appointed officialdom'. Bureaucracy, however, is not the only type of legal domination : 'Parliamentary administration' and 'all sorts of collegial authority and administrative bodies fall into this type'.[49] Collegial bodies, according to Weber, have played an essential role in fostering the legitimate order of the rational state : the concept of constituted 'authorities' has its origin in the power of these agencies. The characteristic problem facing the modern political order is that of reconciling the prevalent demands for 'democratisation', which have been partially developed in former times through the agency of collegial bodies, with the necessarily declining significance of

[48] (1961) p. 252. In traditional China, Weber showed, the absence of a stratum of jurists allowed the 'cultivated' humanism of orthodox Confucianism to become the educational avenue to membership of the state officialdom; similarly, India possessed no group of jurists comparable to those of the West.

[49] 'Die drei reinen Typen der legitimen Herrschaft', in Johannes Winckelmann, *Staatssoziologie* (Berlin, 1966) pp. 100–1.

these bodies – because the era during which real power was vested in such agencies was one in which traditionally established 'notables' (who lived 'for', rather than 'off', politics) were dominant. Modern political forms, which 'are the children of democracy, of mass franchise, of the necessity to woo and organise the masses', entail the formation of bureaucratised parties, whose leaders (who live 'off' politics) hold the real power; thus the power of parliament declines.

Since bureaucracy cannot itself 'lead', but depends upon the setting of objectives from 'outside', political leadership must devolve upon the charismatic properties of the individuals at the head of the party organisations. In thus juxtaposing the rational (bureaucracy) and the irrational (charisma) in the modern political system, Weber's writings express a major line of connection between his general sociology and his specific analysis of German politics. As he insists in his methodological writings, rational analysis cannot validate, or 'disprove', judgements of value. The correlate of this epistemological proposition, in Weber's sociological writings, is that rationalised systems of social organisation do not create values, but instead only function as *means* to the furtherance of existing values. 'This limitation', he made clear, 'is inherent in the legal type at its highest level of development [that is to say, in bureaucratic organisations] because administrative action is limited to what is in conformity with rules.'[50] It is this consideration which underlines Weber's discussion of plebiscitary democracy. While leadership within systems of legal domination can be provided, in the early stages of modern political development, by circles of 'notables', the declining power of such groups with the advance of bureaucracy brings into the sharpest focus the fact that the rationalisation (whether 'intellectual' or 'practical') of conduct can provide only 'means', not 'ends'. Hence the charismatic component previously embodied in the 'hereditary charisma' associated with collegial systems of administration has now to be built upon the emotional

[50] Translation as per *The Theory of Social and Economic Organisation,* p. 392. My parenthesis. This does not mean that bureaucratic officials never use 'initiative', but refers to the moral nature of his 'responsibility' : '. . . to remain outside the realm of the struggle for power – is the official's role . . .' (1968, II 1404).

loyalty between the modern political leader *as a personality* and the mass of his followers. Thus while recognising the potential dangers of Caesarism, Weber was led by the postulates of his own theoretical system to recognise the necessity of the charismatic properties of leadership generated by the mass franchise.

5. CONCLUSION

In terms of the discussion developed in the preceding sections, it becomes possible to unravel some of the principal dilemmas in Weber's political thought. The overriding problem which occupied Weber's political energies was that of the 'leadership question', resulting from Bismarck's domination. Germany is a 'power-state', which has forged its unity in a struggle with the other European nations. In the political conflicts of the nation-states, the unending war of the 'gods', now manifest in the form of 'impersonal powers', continues to hold sway. 'Here . . . ultimate *Weltanschauungen* clash, world-views among which in the end one has to make a choice.'[51] From the earliest phase of his political career, Weber determined his 'choice' : that the values embodied in the German cultural heritage can be defended and furthered only by the acceptance and advancement of the power of the German nation-state. Since those who were the previous bearers of this culture in the political sphere (the *Junker* 'aristocracy') are a declining group, responsibility for political leadership must be derived from other sources. The same processes which have undermined the position of the *Junkers* have furthered the rationalisation of the political order. Weber's general sociological formulation of the relationship between rationalisation and social change involves a polar contrast between the rule-bound character of bureaucracy and the value-creative properties of charisma. Thus the bureaucratisation of political life, while elevating the conduct of human affairs to a peak of technical efficiency, cannot itself generate the capacities involved in 'genuine' leadership. In the democratic order, he saw both the need and the possibility to

[51] (1958a) p. 117.

create the charismatic element necessary to the modern political leader.

It thus follows from Weber's whole analysis that democratic government cannot be founded upon any conception of natural law, such as that embodied in the classical democratic theory of the eighteenth and early nineteenth centuries. Democracy is a technique, a means to an end.[52] In stressing the significance of this point, in his analysis of Weber's political writings, Mommsen is surely correct. But the brutal clarity of Weber's statements on this issue has led to substantial misinterpretation of his political views, in three respects: firstly, in regard to his supposed 'Machiavellianism'; secondly, in relation to his sanctioning of German 'imperialism'; and thirdly, as concerns his 'rejection' of liberalism in favour of a Nietzschean 'aristocratic ethic'. Whatever affinities his writings may have with those of Machiavelli, Weber resolutely avoided any implication that power should be attributed with either the ethical or aesthetic qualities which it has in the latter's conception. As Weber wrote: 'The mere "power politician" may get strong effects, but actually his work leads nowhere and is senseless.'[53] In his view, this is exactly the form of *Realpolitik* which characterised the vacillating policies followed by Germany from the time of Bismarck's downfall. The strength of Weber's commitment to 'imperialism' has been particularly stressed by Marcuse and by Lukács. According to Lukács, democracy is to Weber only a 'technical measure to facilitate a more adequately functioning imperialism . . .'.[54] But as an expression of Weber's views, this is as misleading as that which sees in his political writings nothing more than a new Machiavellianism, and for the same reason: Weber nowhere gave *normative* significance to German expansionism. In Weber's political thought, 'imperialism' (in the same way as 'power' itself) is a means, not an end.

Much of the recent literature on Weber's political writings and involvements (including Mommsen's work) has neglected the strong personal affiliation which he himself felt for the yearnings and the aspirations of the underprivileged. If Weber refused to

[52] In this connection see especially (1958b) pp. 233–79.
[53] (1958a) p. 116.
[54] Lukács (1955) p. 488.

adopt the ethical premisses of democratic theory, his writings are none the less steeped in the traditions of European liberalism. He constantly reaffirmed his advocacy of the values of 'man's personal autonomy' and 'the spiritual and moral values of mankind'.[55] But, within the context of Weber's political sociology, both the rising aspirations of the lower classes, and the tenets of liberal individualism to which he adhered, can only be furthered through the power-interests of the state: 'All culture today is, and will remain, completely tied to the nation. . . .'[56] Moreover, there is a tragic antinomy between the historically closely related values of equality and levelling on the one hand, and individual freedom and spontaneity on the other. The growth of mass politics necessarily limits the degree to which the latter values can be realised in the contemporary social order. Thus Weber saw plebiscitary democracy as the only mode of partially releasing modern man from the 'iron cage' of the bureaucratised division of labour.

If these views are rooted in Weber's assessment of the political structure of Wilhelmine Germany, they are also logically and empirically related to, and were partly shaped by, his methodological conceptions and his studies of the 'world civilisations'. Weber spoke in the language of his contemporaries when he talked of the 'power-interests' of the nation and of the *Herrenvolk*. But his usage of these notions, especially in his later writings, was in very definite respects quite different from that of the sources from which he adopted this terminology. In the first place, he rejected the emphasis upon the state *itself* as the ultimate value in his personal political objectives. While there is still an ambiguity in Weber's position on this matter in the *Antrittsrede*, in his subsequent writings this is quite clear. In the 'nation-state', it is the first half of the conjunction which is significant in Weber's personal scale of values. Secondly, Weber did not utilise the term *Herrenvolk* in a way which carried the connotation that German culture can claim a 'legitimate' domination over that of other nations. On the contrary, in Weber's view such a claim is both factually invalid and (which is a logically separate question) normatively rejected. The political struggle of nation-states is a

[55] Quoted in Marianne Weber (1950) p. 159.
[56] (1958*b*) p. 47.

sphere of power relations; and the values comprised in the national culture of these states cannot be adjudged as 'ethically' superior to German culture.

Weber's epistemological conception of the 'ethical irrationality' of the world, and the methodological apparatus which he constructed upon this basis, involves an attempt to integrate various diverse tendencies in German social thought. Rejecting both 'intuitionism' and 'scientism', he borrowed elements from each in elaborating a framework which hinges upon certain antinomies between the 'rational' and the 'irrational', and between the 'subjective' and 'objective'. As has been indicated in Section 4 of this study, these underlie the sociological conceptions which Weber both developed as a set of 'pure categories' and applied empirically in his studies of history and society. These conceptions involve the notion that all human actions which approximate to rationality (in either of Weber's two principal senses) *must* necessarily be grounded in irrationality ('ultimate values'); but that there is a fundamental dichotomy between reason and value. Hence sociology and history must entail recourse to the interpretation of 'meaning', but sociological or historical analysis cannot 'prove' any given set of values to be normatively 'valid'.

In Weber's typology of domination, these two emphases are built into the conception of charisma. Charisma is irrational in the sense of being foreign to rule-bound action, and is therefore the value-creative force in history; and the concept, as he formulates it, completely cross-cuts all differences in the *content* of charismatic attachments, such that Hitler is as 'genuine' a charismatic leader as is Gandhi. Hence, in Weber's thought, the notion of 'value' becomes synonymous with (irrational) conviction; his conceptual categories, in this respect, bear no direct relation to 'egoism' and 'altruism' as these are traditionally conceived in ethical theory. In Weber's analysis of German politics, what in the *Antrittsrede* is seen as the 'leadership problem' came to be analysed in the later political writings as turning upon the opposition between bureaucratic rationality and charisma. Thus Weber was inevitably led towards the conclusion that the *content* of the charismatic element is irrelevant to what he consciously took as his own ultimate value (the autonomous furtherance of German culture). This, conjoined with his analysis of the bureau-

57

cratisation entailed in the modern capitalist state, brought him into a position in which the liberal democratic values which he was drawn to could at most be conceived as a 'means', and therefore as denuded of intrinsic significance.

Weber's political thought thus conceals an inherent tension, which gives his writings their strongly defined character of pathos. On the one hand, he expressed sympathies with certain of the tenets of classical liberalism and even socialism; but both his starting-point in politics (as set out in the *Antrittsrede*), and the intellectual standpoint which he elaborated in his academic writings, directed his views towards a position in which, as he himself put it, 'such concepts as the "will of the people", the true will of the people . . . are *fictions*'.[57] A short while before he died, he remarked that Marx and Nietzsche represent the two dominant influences in modern culture. The whole corpus of Weber's works could be said to constitute a grandiose attempt to integrate the most profound insights of these two seemingly incompatible streams of thought. His political views both helped to form, and were formed by, this massive, but brittle, intellectual synthesis, and they share the dualities which it embodies.

A satisfactory critique of Weber's political sociology must itself be both political and intellectual. That it is to say, it must examine, in detail, as related questions, the dependence of his ideas upon a specific historical context, and the logical weaknesses of his theoretical formulations. Such a critique has not, thus far, emerged from the continuing debate over his political writings. Marxist critics of Weber, on the one side, have tended to treat his sociological writings as little more than ideological expressions of his political interests. Weber's sociology is, absurdly, reduced largely to a particular manifestation of 'bourgeois culture' in Wilhelmine Germany. On the other side, the 'orthodox' interpreters of Weber defend the view that his academic contributions to social science are to be treated as quite separable from his political attachments. But these positions, at least in the extreme

[57] Quoted in Mommsen (1959) pp. 392–3. This sort of statement has to be read in juxtaposition with Weber's conviction that 'it is a gross self-deception to believe that without the achievements of the age of the Rights of Man any one of us, including the most conservative, can go on living his life' (1968, III 1403).

form in which they have sometimes been stated, simply obstruct an adequate evaluation of Weber's work, a task which is still of considerable importance to modern sociology. For each of these states something which is little more than a truism; it must be true of any major social thinker that his work is expressive of the particular social and political context in which he lived, but also embodies conceptions which are capable of generalised application.

BIBLIOGRAPHY

I have weighted this bibliography towards English-language sources; much of the relevant literature, however, is only available in German.

Carlo Antoni, *From History to Sociology* (London, 1962). A brilliantly succinct account of what the author, a follower of Croce, regards as the 'decline' of German historical thought into sociology. Analyses not only Weber, but also Dilthey, Troeltsch, Meinecke, Huizinga, and Wölfflin. Can be usefully contrasted with Lukács's work (see below).

Eduard Baumgarten (ed.), *Max Weber, Werk und Person* (Tübingen, 1964). A valuable and well-ordered collection of selections from Weber's writings, including personal documents.

Reinhard Bendix, *Max Weber: An Intellectual Portrait* (London, 1966). The best general survey of Weber's works on sociology, economics and history. Includes lengthy analyses of Weber's studies of the 'world religions'.

Arnold Bergstraesser, 'Max Webers Antrittsvorlesung in zeitgeschichtlicher Perspektive', *Vierteljahrshefte für Zeitgeschichte*, v (1957). A recent discussion of Weber's Freiburg inaugural lecture, placing particular emphasis upon the historical context influencing the ideas set out therein.

Eugène Fleischmann, 'De Weber à Nietzsche', *Archives Européennes de Sociologie*, v (1964). A study of the influence of Nietzsche upon Weber's thought. An interesting and informed discussion, but exaggerates the degree to which Weber moved 'away' from Marx towards Nietzsche.

Julien Freund, *The Sociology of Max Weber* (London, 1968). A sound and clear exposition of the main themes in Weber's work. Gives some attention to indicating the relationship between Weber's methodological views and his more empirical writings.

Anthony Giddens, *Capitalism and Modern Social Theory* (Cambridge, 1971). Includes lengthy discussions of the work of Marx and Durkheim as well as of Weber. Gives particular attention to the relationship between Marx and Weber.

——, 'Marx, Weber, and the Development of Capitalism', *Sociology,* IV (1970). A summary version of some of the points made at greater length in the work above.

Dieter Lindenlaub, *Richtungskämpfe im Verein für Sozialpolitik* (Wiesbaden, 1967). An extremely important and detailed study of the debates among the members of the *Verein für Sozialpolitik.* Provides material upon the influence of Marxism upon Weber and his contemporaries, and analyses their divergent treatments of capitalism and socialism.

Karl Loewenstein, *Max Weber's Political Ideas in the Perspective of our Time* (Amherst, Mass., 1966). An attempt to examine the contemporary relevance of Weber's political ideas. Rather banal, but constitutes one of the few general accounts of Weber's political views available in English.

Karl Löwith, 'Max Weber und Karl Marx', *Archiv für Sozialwissenschaft und Sozialpolitik,* LXVII (1932). A classic comparative analysis of similarities and divergencies between the views of Marx and Weber. Written shortly after the first publication of Marx's 'early writings', it provides what is one of the most incisive and perceptive comparisons of the ideas of the two thinkers.

Georg Lukács, *Die Zerstörung der Vernunft* (Berlin, 1955). A major attempt to interpret the trend of development in German philosophy and sociology during the period of German 'imperialism'. Written from a Marxist standpoint, the study seeks to expose the fundamental irrationalism which Lukács believes to characterise German social thought from the late eighteenth century onwards.

J. P. Mayer, *Max Weber and German Politics* (London, 1956). Initially published in 1944, this was the first general account of Weber's political thought to appear in English. While it bears a strong imprint of the time at which it was written, it is still a useful account.

Arthur Mitzman, *The Iron Cage: An Historical Interpretation of Max Weber* (New York, 1970). A well-documented 'psychological biography' of Weber. Departs considerably from the standard biography by Marianne Weber (see below).

Wolfgang J. Mommsen, *Max Weber und die deutsche Politik, 1890–1920* (Tübingen, 1959). The most detailed and comprehensive study of Weber's political writings and activities which has yet appeared. Employing a considerable number of previously unpublished letters and fragments left by Weber, it is an essential source.

——, 'Max Weber's Political Sociology and his Philosophy of World History', *International Social Science Journal*, XVII (1965). A general discussion of points of interrelationship between Weber's political and sociological writings.

Talcott Parsons, 'Capitalism in Recent German Literature: Sombart and Weber', *Journal of Political Economy*, XXXVI (1928). A useful analysis of the importance of the conception of 'capitalism' in the work of Sombart and Weber. Can be profitably compared with Lindenlaub (see above).

——, *The Structure of Social Action* (Glencoe, Ill., 1949). An extremely influential discussion of Weber, within the framework of an analysis of a presumed 'convergence' of thought between Marshall, Pareto, Durkheim and Weber.

Günther Roth, 'Political Critiques of Max Weber: Some Implications for Political Sociology', *American Sociological Review*, XXX (1965). A short overall account of some of the main avenues of critical attack to which Weber's political views have been subject. Highly critical of 'ideological' attacks on Weber, the article itself ends on a strongly ideological note.

——, *The Social Democrats in Imperial Germany* (Englewood Cliffs, N.J., 1963). The best general study of the development of Social Democracy in Wilhelmine Germany; includes a good deal of material on Weber, and a discussion of his relationship to Michels.

Gustav Schmidt, *Deutscher Historismus und der Übergang zur parlamentarischen Demokratie* (Lübeck and Hamburg. 1964). A study covering some of the principal political thinkers in the Wilhelmine period. Includes a lengthy section on Weber's political views.

Otto Stammler (ed.), *Max Weber and Sociology Today* (Oxford, 1971). Conference papers from the 1964 meetings of the German Sociological Association, held to commemorate the centenary of Weber's birth. Documents the controversy over papers by Raymond Aron and Herbert Marcuse on Weber's political thought.

Marianne Weber, *Max Weber: ein Lebensbild* (Heidelberg, 1950). Marianne Weber's biography of her husband, although having been shown to contain certain important inaccuracies, is still a most basic source-book on Weber's political views.

Max Weber, *Economy and Society*, 3 vols (New York, 1968). Although intended only as a schematic introduction to a collection of volumes on economics and sociology, and remaining uncompleted, this massive work represents the summation of Weber's contributions to sociology. Vol. III of the English translation includes as an appendix 'Parliament and Government in a Reconstructed Germany'.

——, *From Max Weber: Essays in Sociology,* ed. H. H. Gerth and C. Wright Mills (New York, 1958a). An extremely useful selection from Weber's writings, which includes Weber's famous lecture 'Politics as a Vocation', as well as two or three other writings of an immediately political character.

——, *General Economic History* (New York, 1961). Mainly reconstructed from students' notes, this book is nevertheless important, because it offers the only place in which there is something approaching a general analysis of the conditions Weber believed to be most relevant to the explanation of the emergence of Western capitalism.

——, *Gesammelte politische Schriften* (Tübingen, 1958*b*). The standard collected edition of Weber's political writings.

——, *The Methodology of the Social Sciences* (Glencoe, Ill., 1949). Translations of three of Weber's essays on the philosophy and method of social science.

Johannes Winckelmann, *Legitimität und Legalität in Max Webers Herrschaftssoziologie* (Tübingen, 1952). An analysis of the much-debated issue of the relationship between 'legitimacy' and 'legality' in Weber's political sociology. A critique of Winckelmann's interpretation is given in Mommsen's *Max Weber und die deutsche Politik* (see above).